VIOLA
86VA

FINE TUNING

50 INTERMEDIATE STRING ENSEMBLES FOR DEVELOPING SOLID INTONATION & TONE PRODUCTION

ARRANGED BY
FRANK SPINOSA & HAROLD W. RUSCH

Welcome to **FINE TUNING!** Inside you will find a collection of 50 short pieces which have been compiled and arranged for string ensembles of all sizes. It features a wide variety of music offering many opportunities to improve and strengthen intonation. With solid intonation, musicians can further work to achieve a cohesive ensemble sound by practicing on tone and balance. Positive reinforcement of these skills will bring many rewards for not only the group as a whole, but for you as an individual.

ISBN 0-8497-3260-3

CONTENTS

D Major/b minor

1 Chorale .... Johann Sebastian Bach *(1685-1750)* 3
2 America .... Henry Carey *(1687-1743)* 3
3 Presto Pizzicato .... Anonymous 3
4 The Conquering Hero .... George Frederic Handel *(1685-1759)* 4
5 Royal March .... Charles Rinck *(1770-1846)* 4
6 Chorale .... Robert Lowry *(1826-1899)* 4
7 Jubilee .... Johann Herzog *(1822-1909)* 5
8 Intrade .... Charles Rinck *(1770-1846)* 5

G Major/e minor

9 Chorale .... Robert Schumann *(1810-1856)* 5
10 Little Song in G .... Adolf Friedrich Hesse *(1809-1863)* 6
11 The Fox Comes to Town .... Traditional Folk Song 6
12 Chanson .... Licio Bottazzo *(1845-1924)* 6
13 Fanfare .... John Jenkins *(1592-1678)* 7
14 Ode to Chautauqua .... William F. Sherwin *(1826-1888)* 7
15 Trust in Thee .... Johann Sebastian Bach *(1685-1750)* 8
16 Con Fervore .... Robert Schumann *(1810-1856)* 8

C Major/a minor

17 St. Antony Chorale .... Franz Joseph Haydn *(1732-1809)* 9
18 The Chase .... adpt. Georg Rosenstengel *(1852-1907)* 9
19 Promenade .... Peter Piel *(1786-1862)* 10
20 Prelude .... Joseph Bernards *(1710-1763)* 10
21 Sailor's Song .... Edvard Grieg *(1843-1907)* 10
22 Aria .... Richard Wagner *(1813-1883)* 11
23 Song of Victory .... Johann Sebastian Bach *(1685-1750)* 11

F Major/d minor

24 Noble Processional .... Anonymous 12
25 Beyond the River .... William Howard Doane *(1832-1915)* 12
26 Fugue .... Johann Sebastian Bach *(1685-1750)* 12
27 Dialogue .... Georg Philipp Telemann *(1681-1767)* 13
28 Trek .... Jacques de la Presle *(1888-1932)* 13
29 Noblesse .... George Frederic Handel *(1685-1759)* 14
30 Air .... Arcangelo Corelli *(1653-1713)* 14
31 Canon .... Henry Purcell *(1659-1695)* 15

B♭ Major/g minor

32 Pastorale .... George Frederic Handel *(1685-1759)* 16
33 Stately .... adpt. John Jenkins *(1592-1678)* 16
34 Hornpipe .... Jacob Sachs *(1830-1888)* 17
35 Sarabande .... Franz Walczynski *(1852-1905)* 17
36 Follow the Leader .... adpt. Charles Rinck *(1770-1846)* 18

A Major/f♯ minor

37 Austrian National Anthem .... Franz Joseph Haydn *(1732-1809)* 18
38 Postlude .... Jacob Sachs *(1830-1888)* 18
39 Divertimento .... Johann Georg Clement *(1710-1794)* 19
40 Chorale .... Johann Sebastian Bach *(1685-1750)* 19
41 Allegro .... Franz Walczynski *(1852-1905)* 19

E♭ Major/c minor

42 Quiet Song .... Orlando Gibbons *(1583-1625)* 20
43 Russian National Hymn .... Alexis F. Lvov *(1798-1870)* 20
44 Passion Chorale .... Johann Sebastian Bach *(1685-1750)* 20
45 Prelude .... Frederic Chopin *(1810-1849)* 20

E Major/c♯ minor

46 Song of Thanksgiving .... J. A. P. Schulz *(1774-1800)* 21
47 Pietoso .... Johannes Brahms *(1833-1897)* 21
48 Morning Prayer .... Peter I. Tchaikovsky *(1840-1893)* 21
49 Furry Day Carol .... Traditional Folk Song 22
50 Arioso .... Jacob Blied *(1844-1884)* 22

D Major/b minor

1

Bach

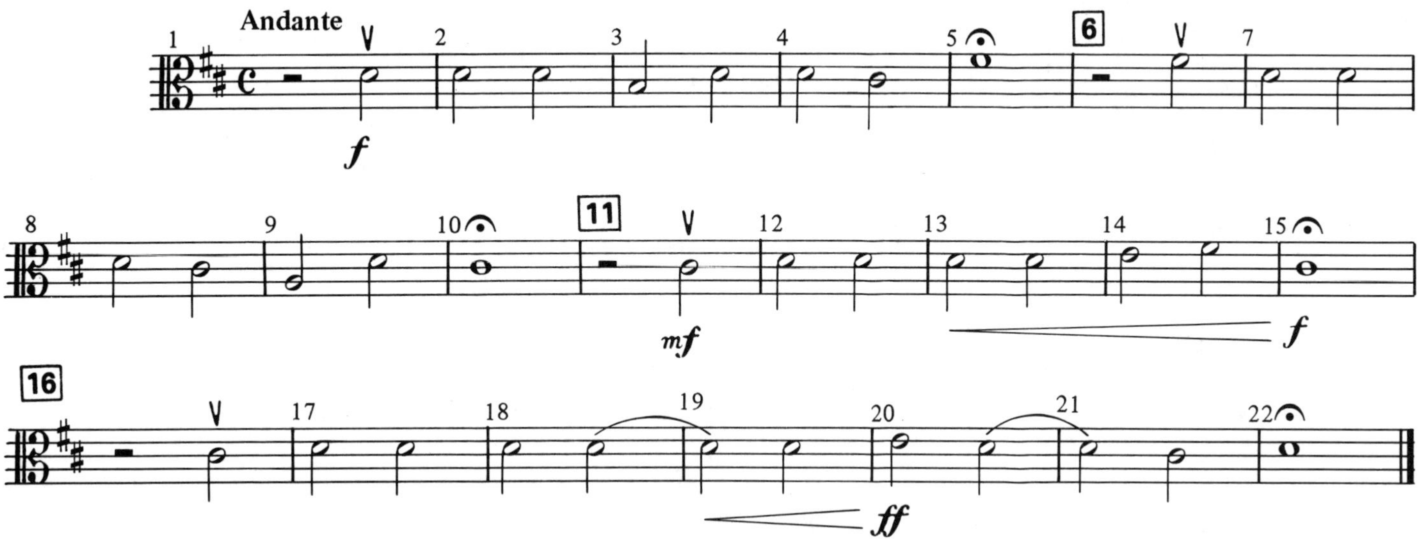

2

Carey

3

Anonymous

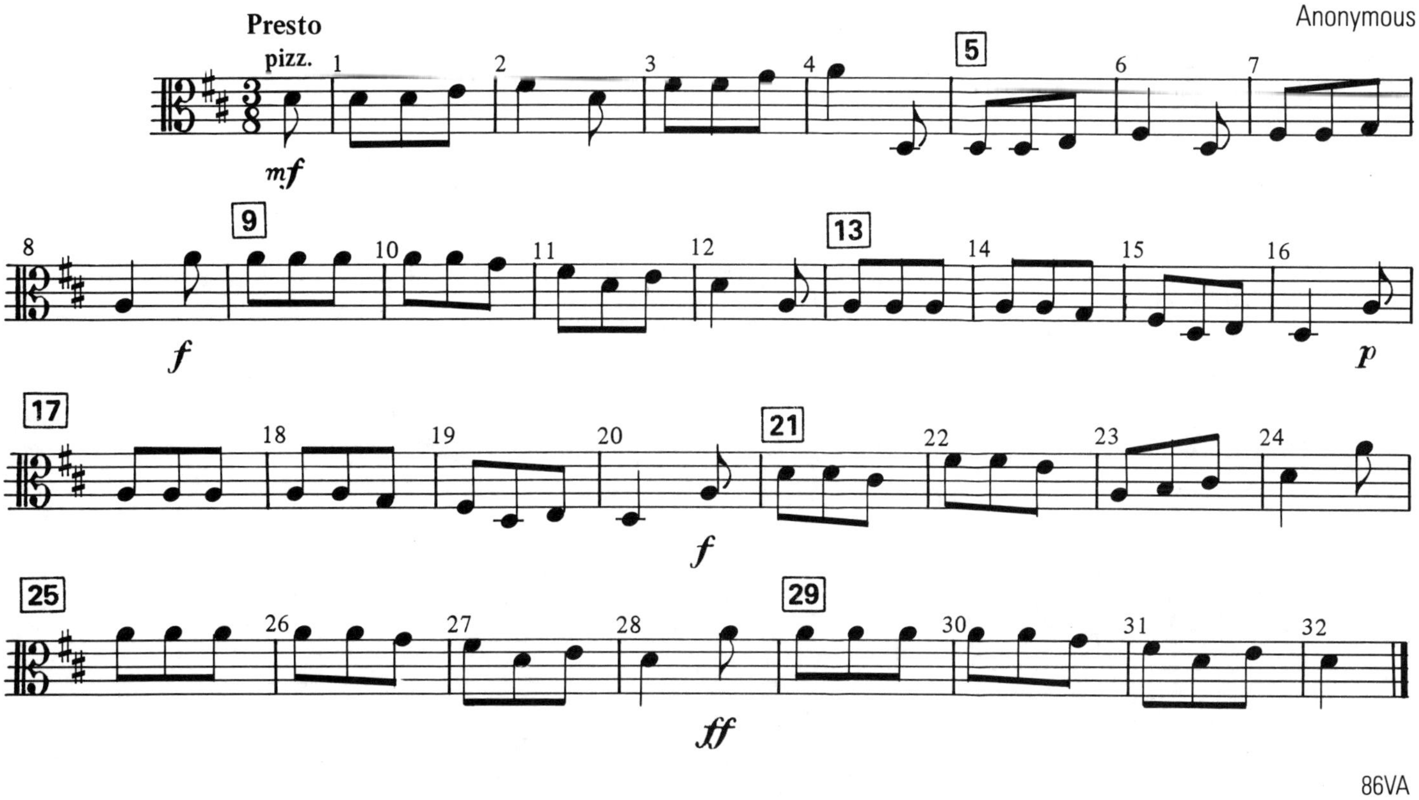

4

Handel

5

Rinck

6

Lowry

7

Herzog

8

Rinck

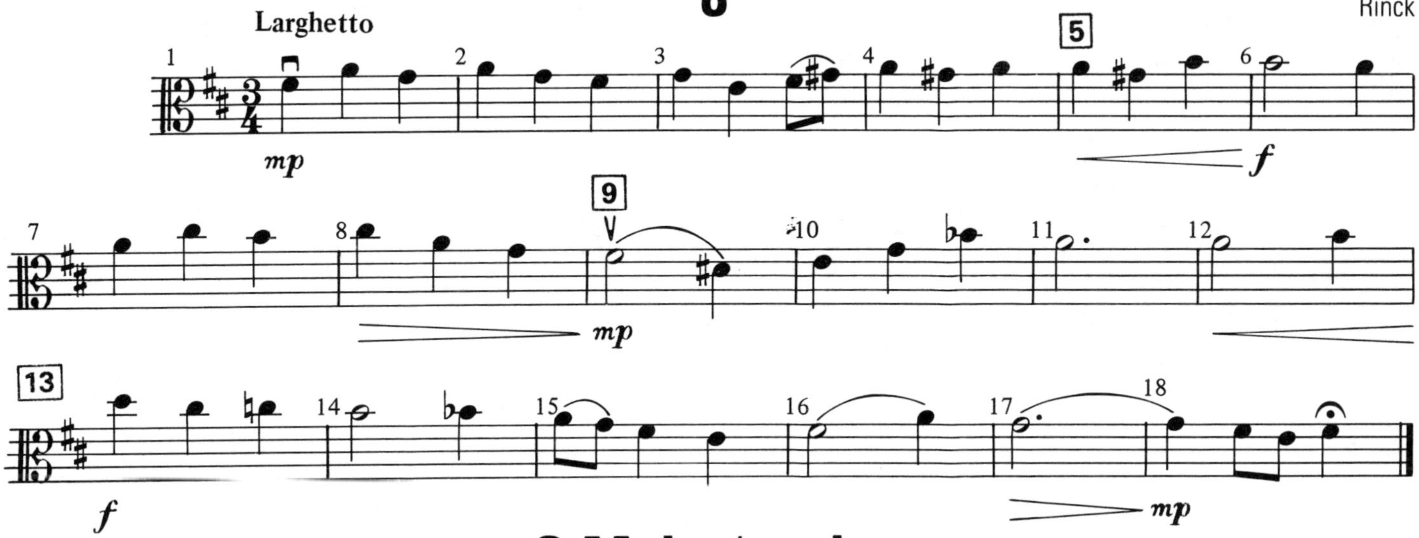

G Major/e minor

9

Schumann

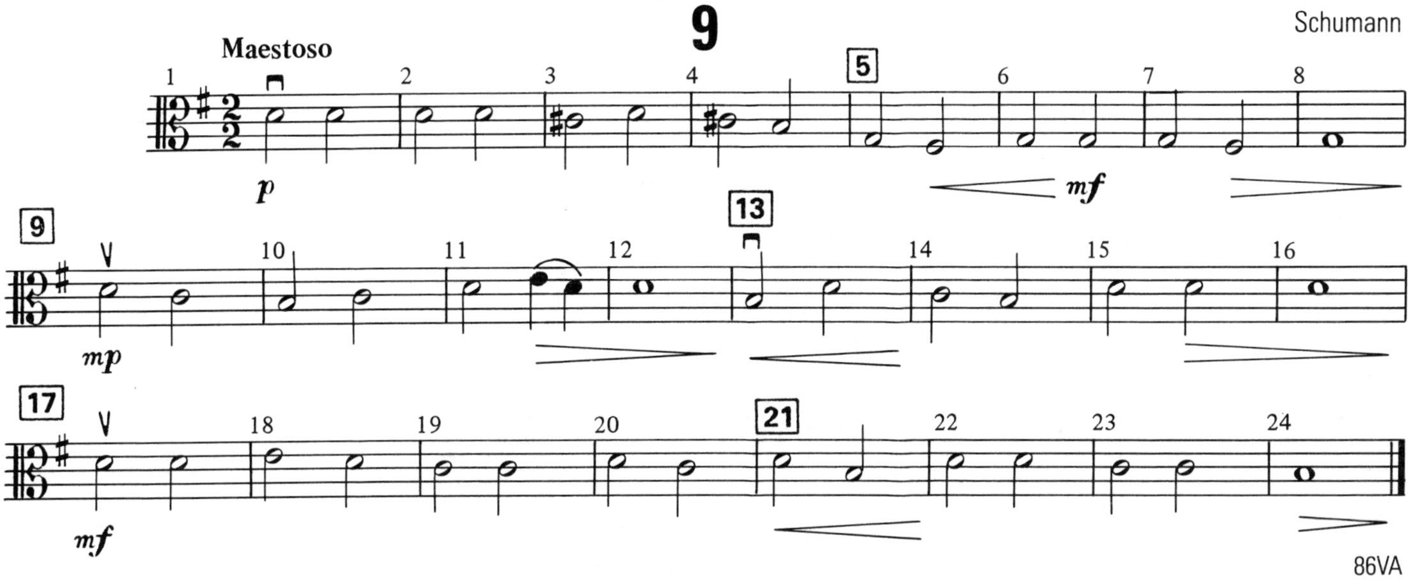

10

Hesse

Moderato

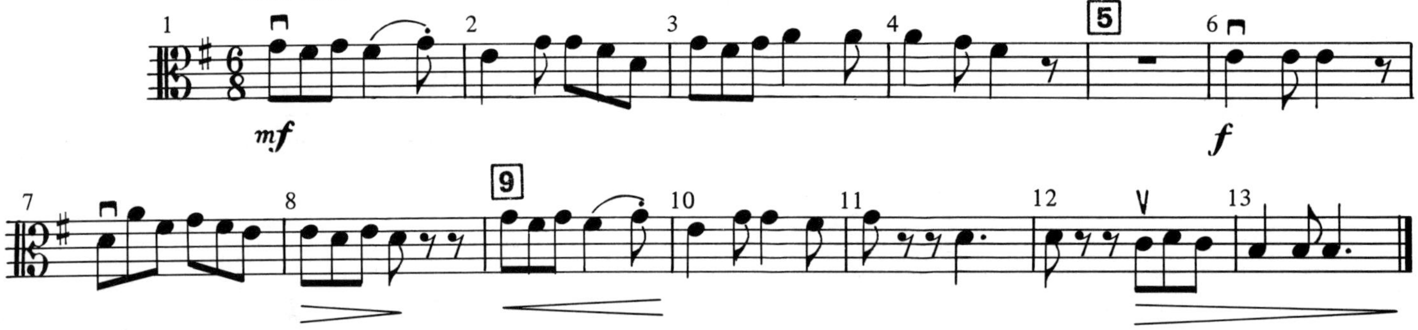

11

Traditional

Very fast

12

Bottazzo

Allegretto

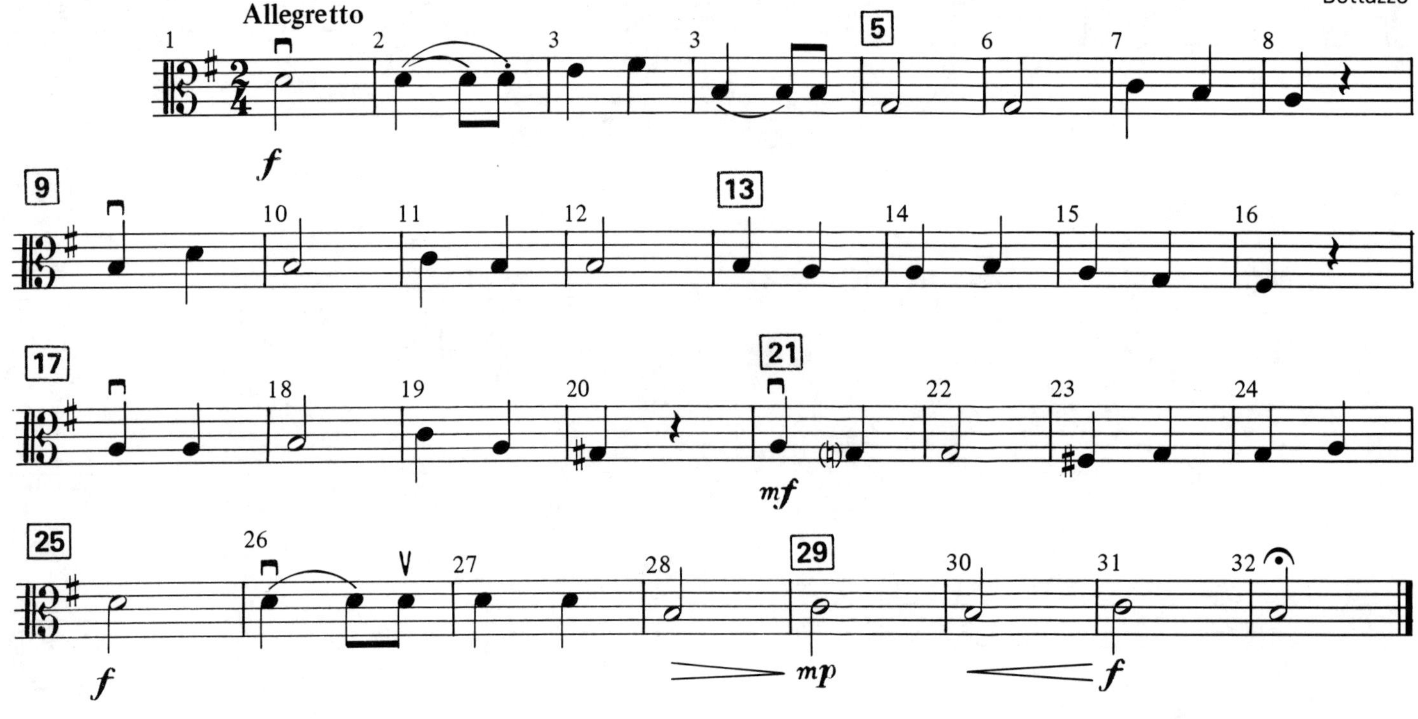

13

Jenkins

14

Sherwin

15

Bach

16

Schumann

C Major/a minor

17

Haydn

18

adpt. Rosenstengel

19

Piel

20

Bernards

21

Grieg

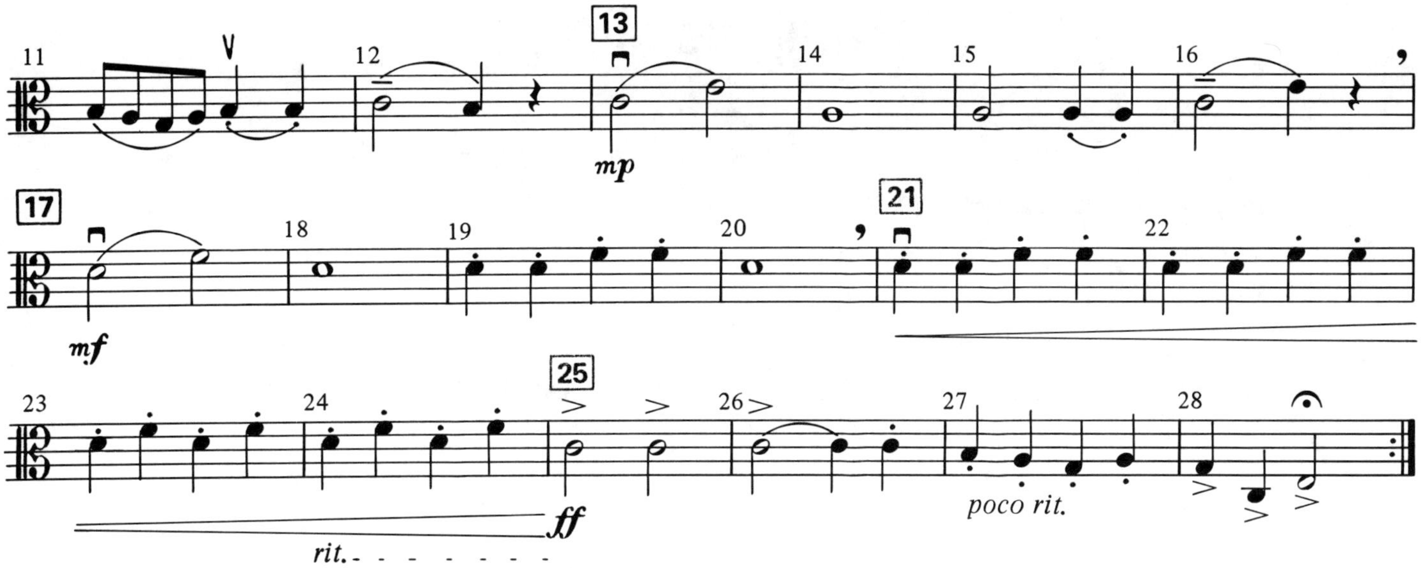

22

Wagner

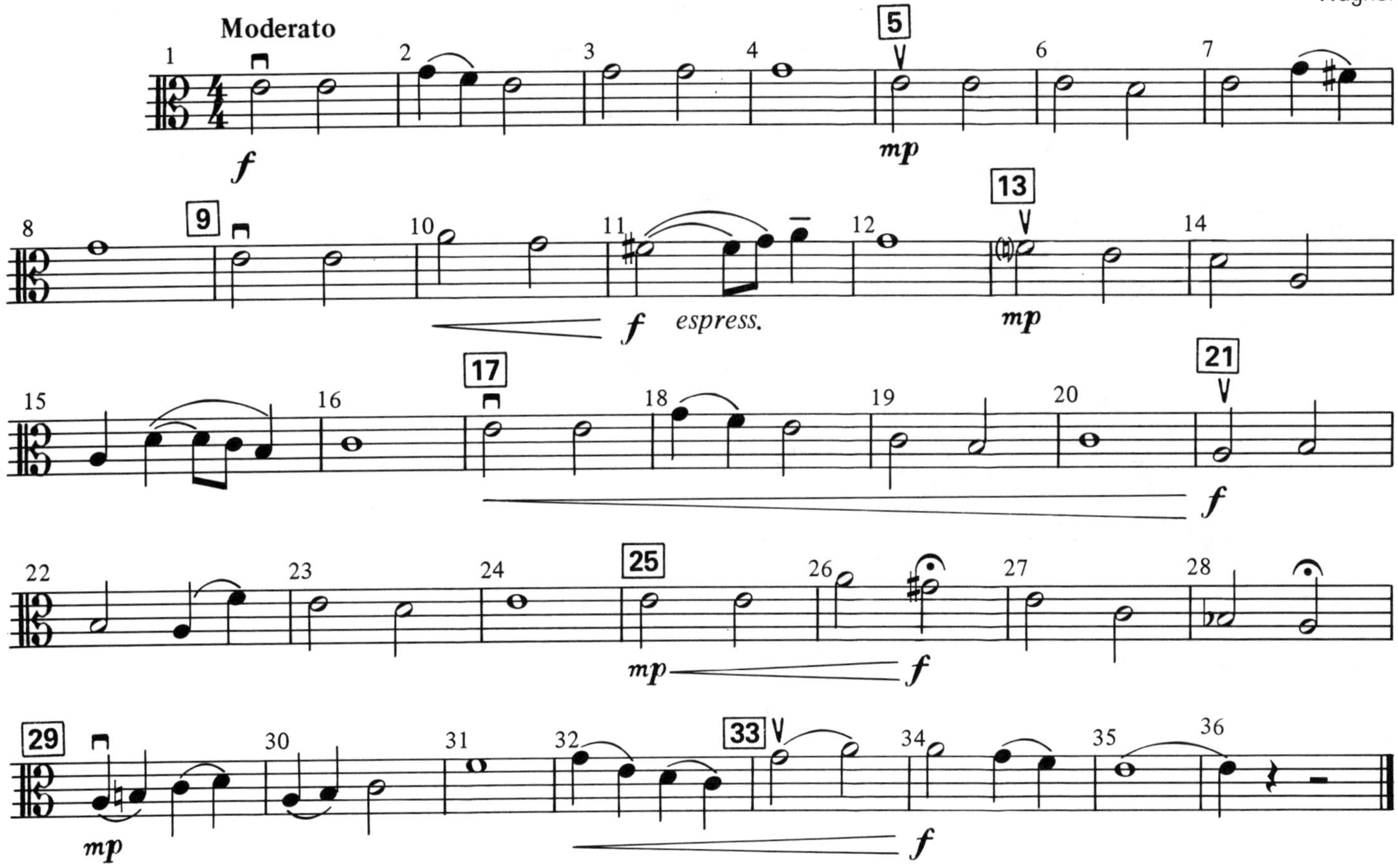

23

Bach

F Major/d minor

24

Anonymous

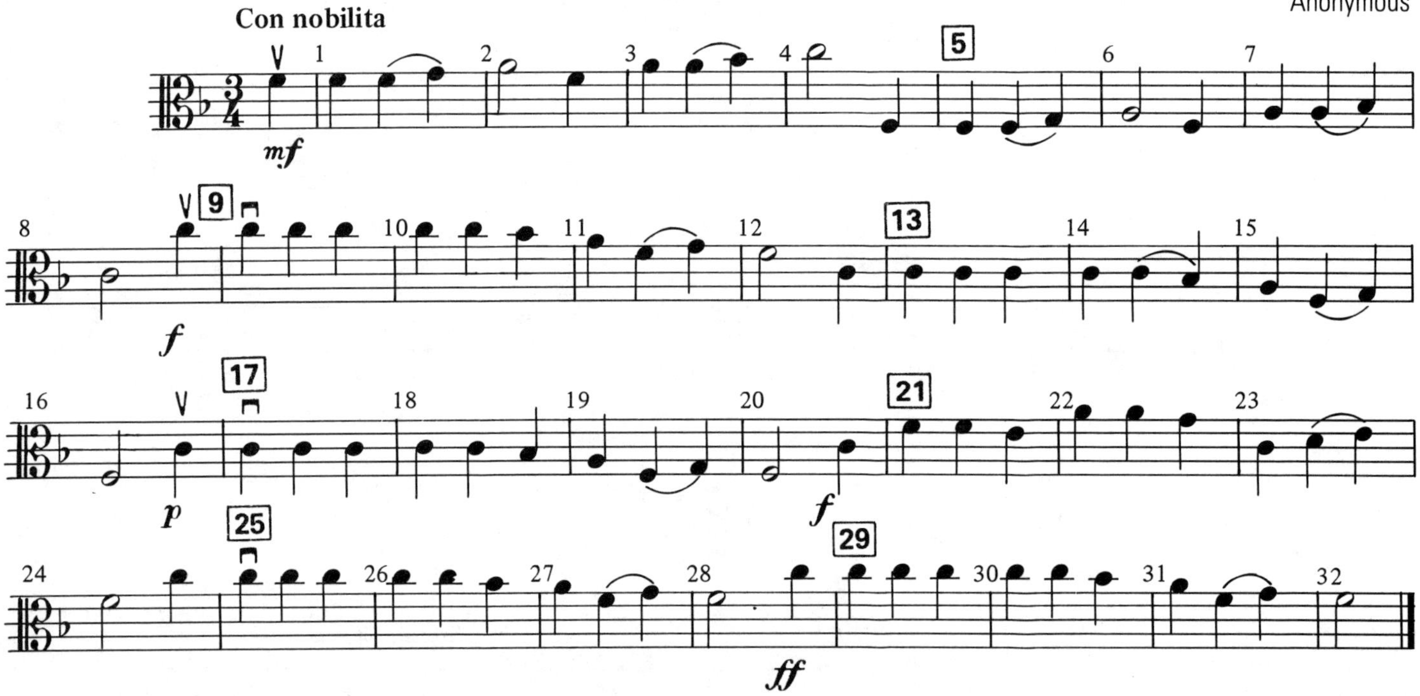

25

Doane

26

Bach

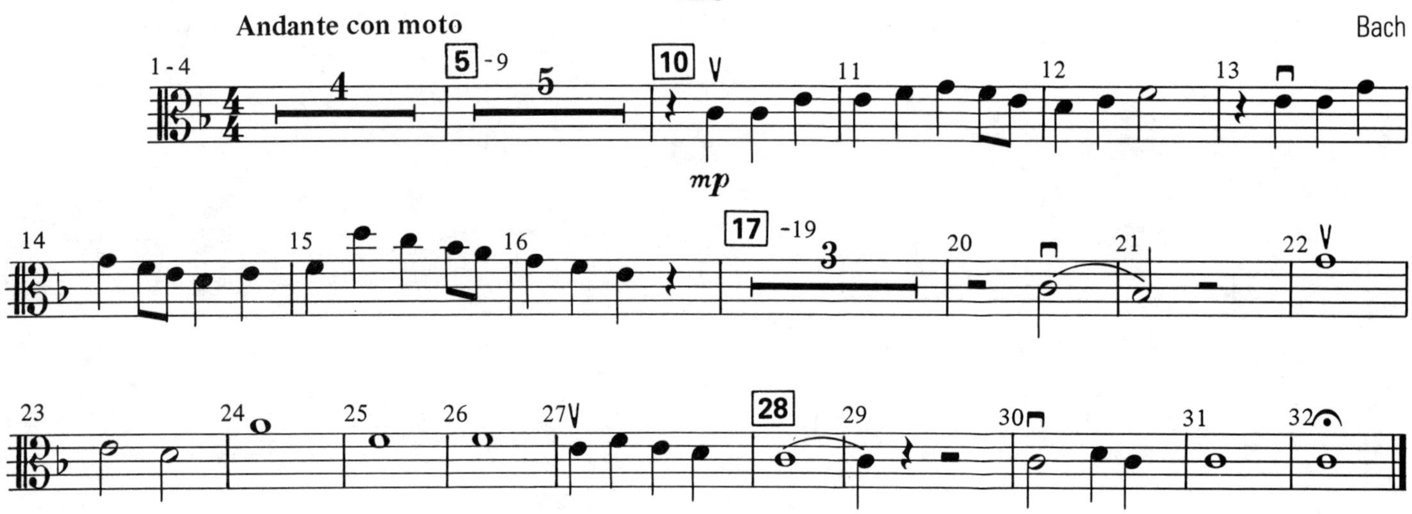

27

Telemann

28

de la Presle

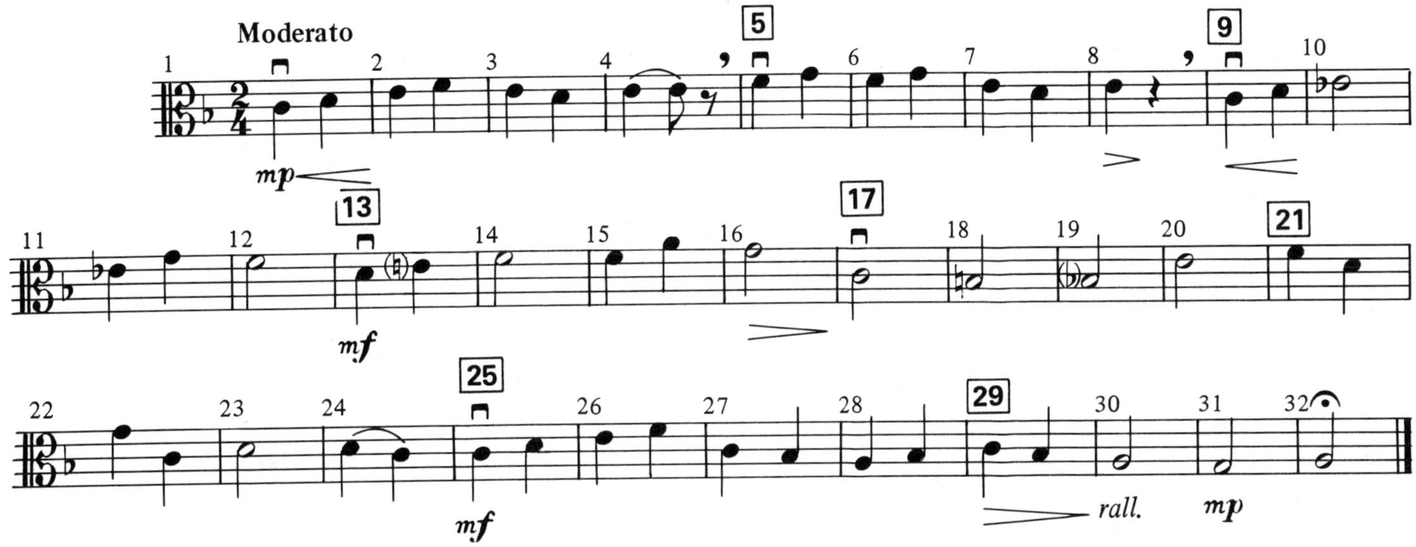

29

Handel

Moderately slow

30

Corelli

Largo

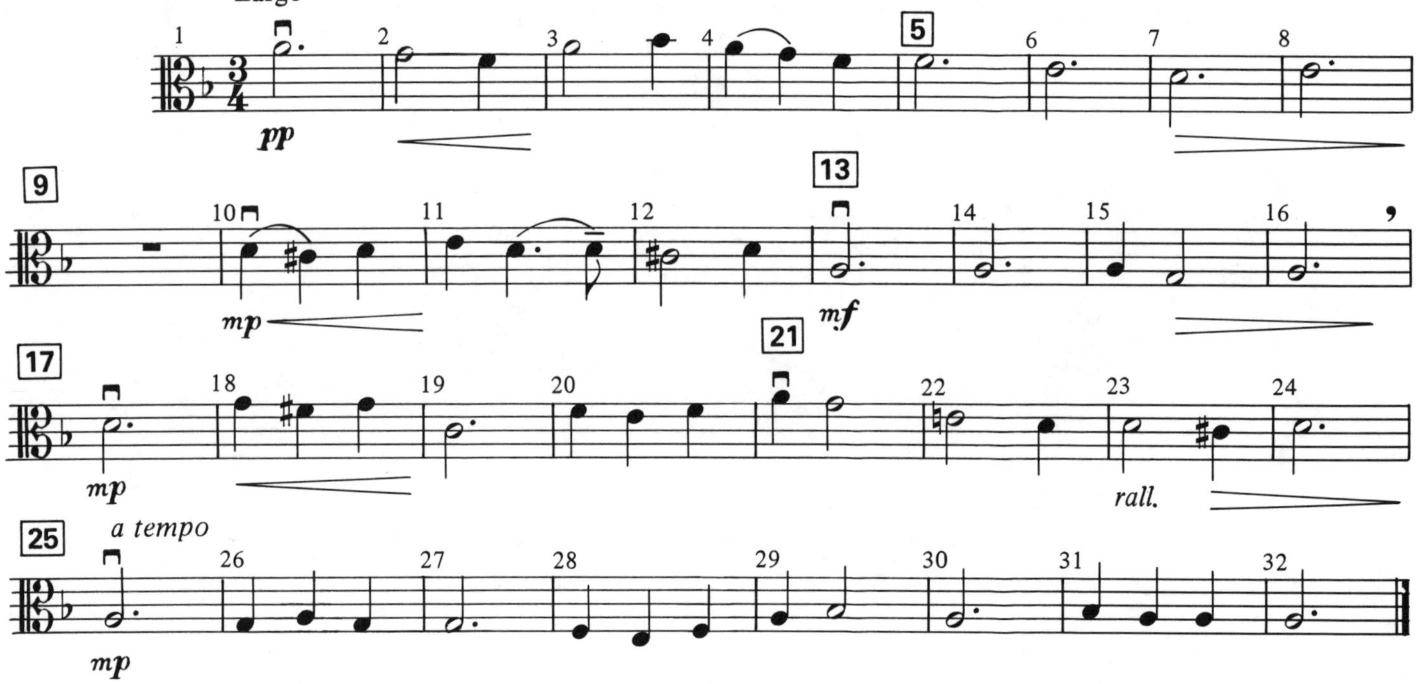

31

Purcell

Allegro non troppo
mf con ritmo e marcato
mp
p
f
div.
allarg. e cresc.
ff

B♭ Major/g minor

32

Handel

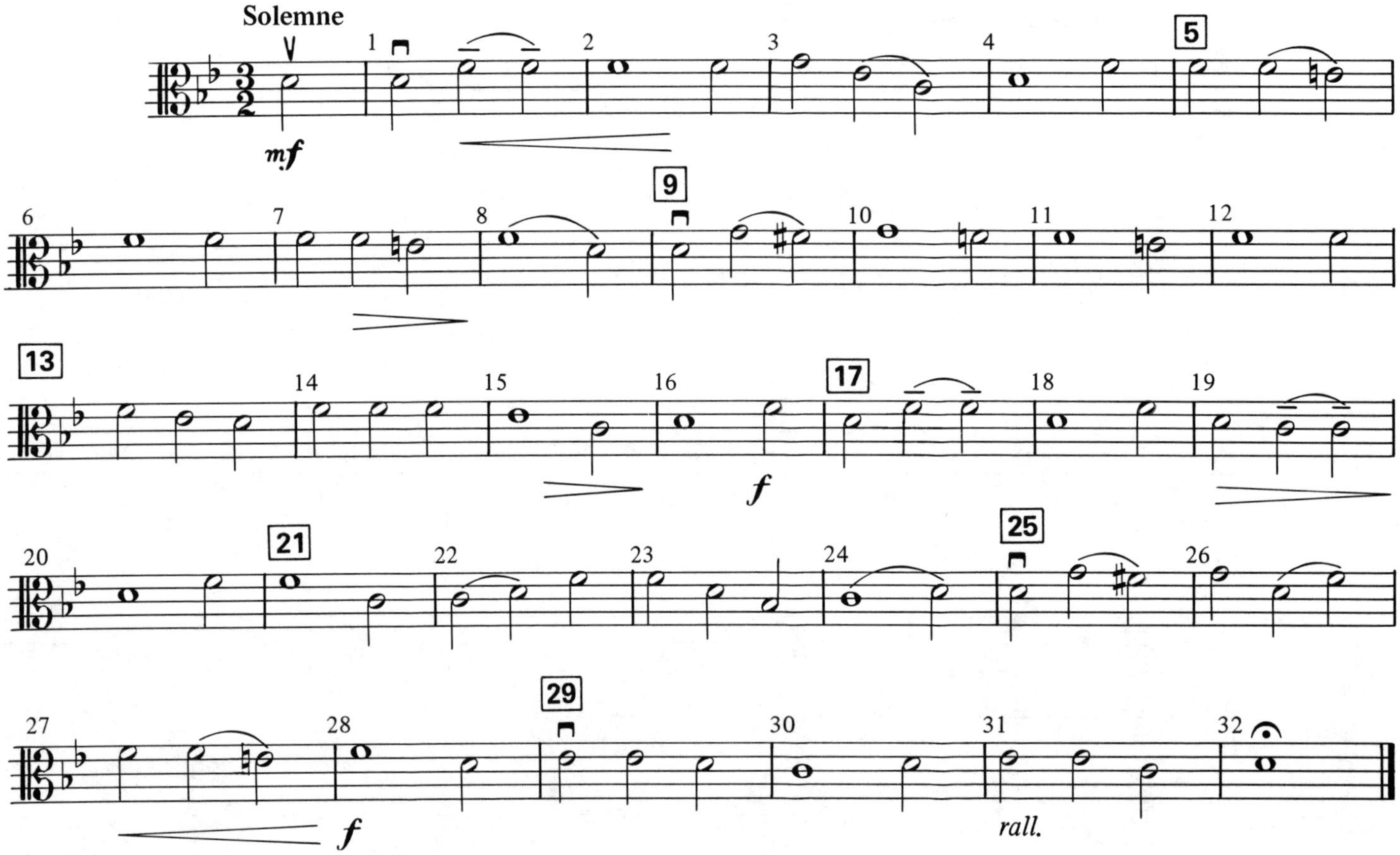

33

adpt. Jenkins

34

Sachs

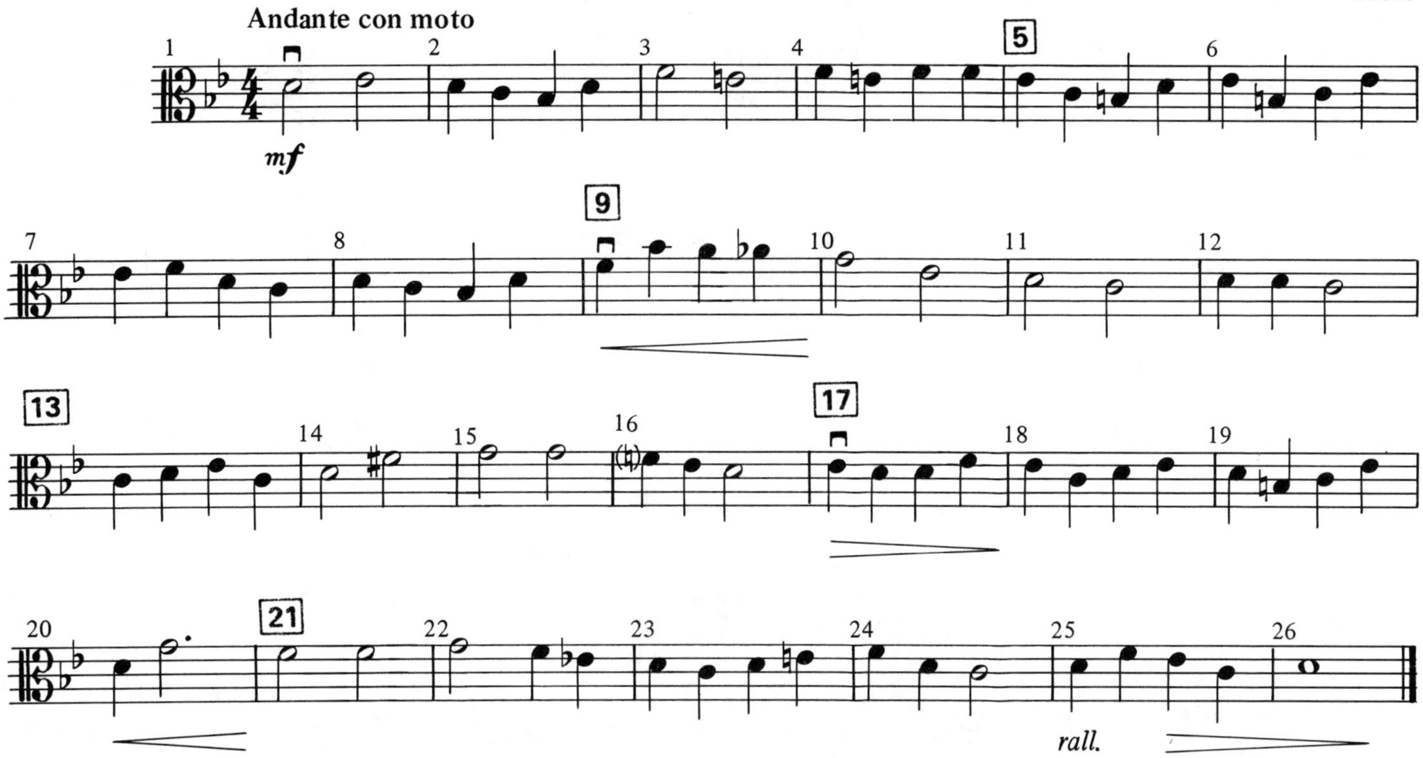

35

Walczynski

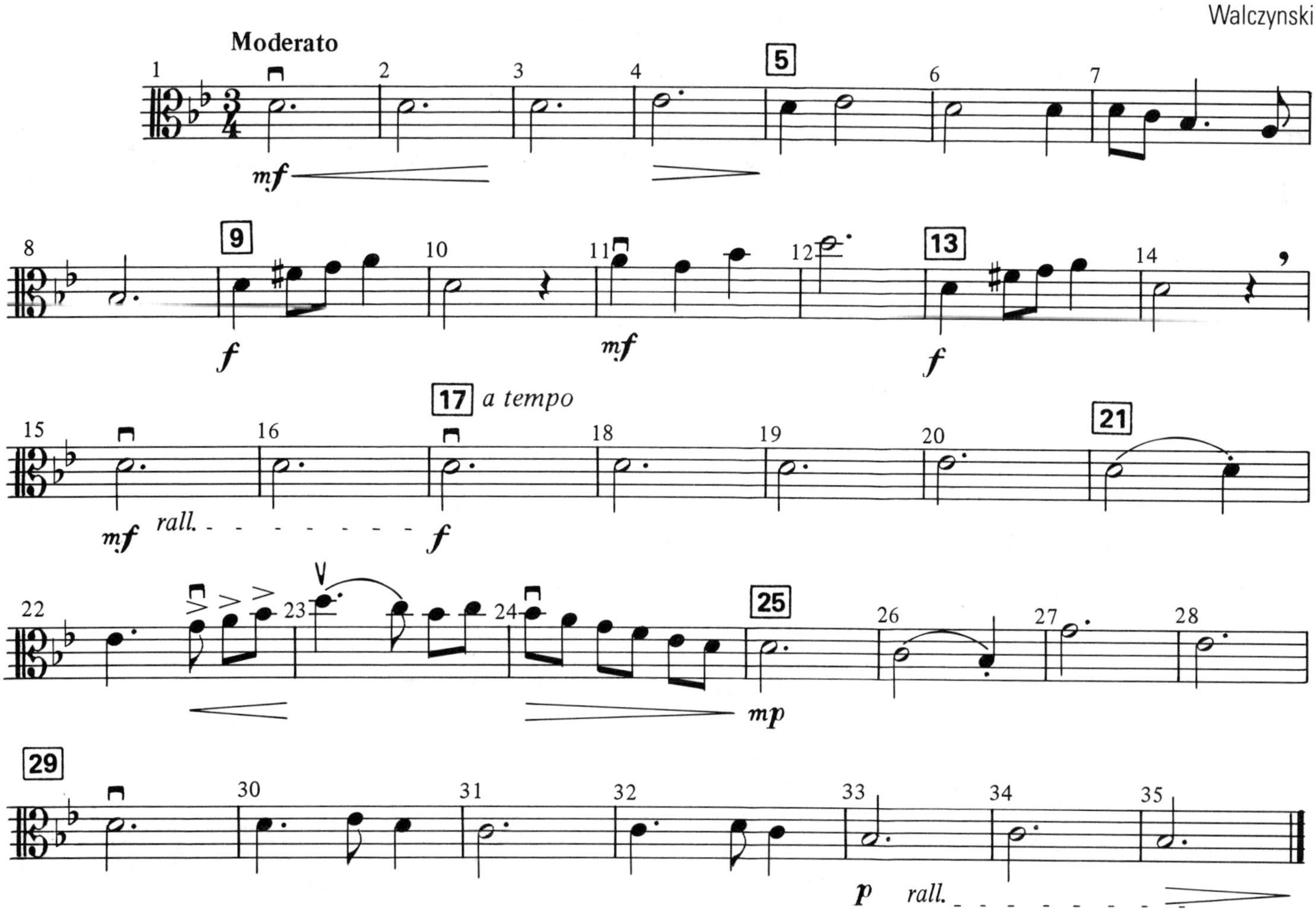

36

adpt. Rinck

A Major/f♯ minor

37

Haydn

38

Sachs

39

Clement

40

Bach

41

Walczynski

E♭ Major/c minor

42

Gibbons

43

Lvov

44

Bach

45

Chopin

E Major/c♯ minor

46

Allegro energico

Schulz

47

Pietoso

Brahms

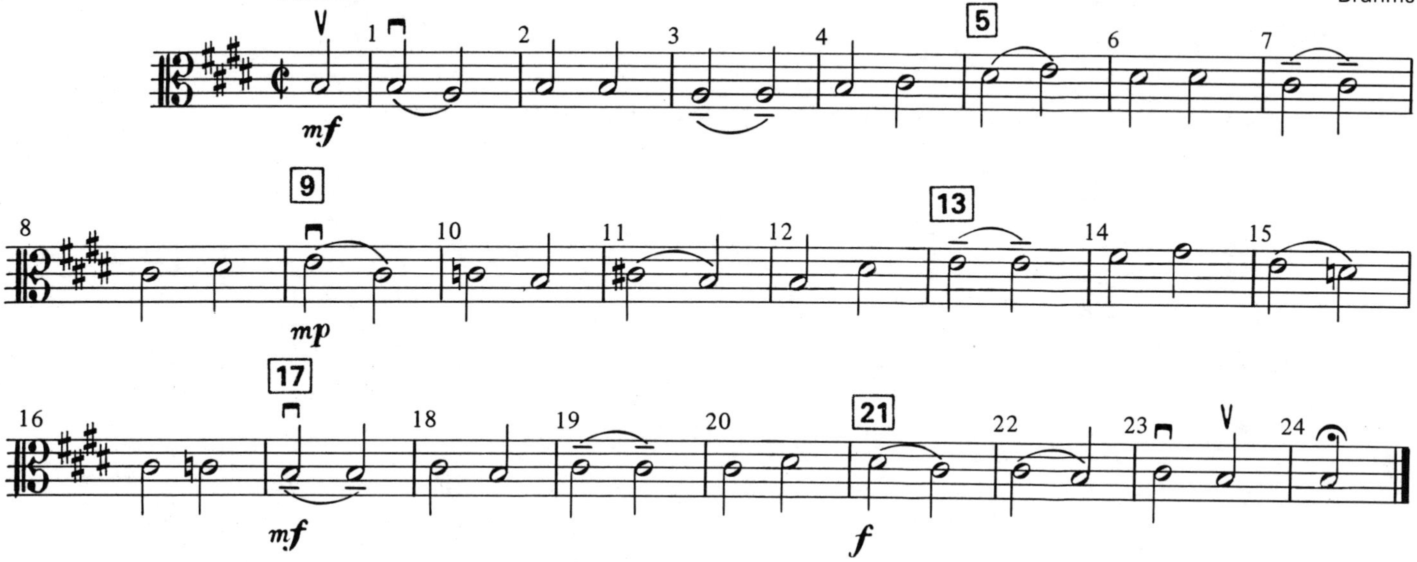

48

Flowing

Tchaikovsky

49

Traditional

50

Blied